THE SEWING
MACHINE MAN

ALAN BAMBER

For Dad.

Thanks to my editor, Katherine Trail, and illustrator, Maria Dalbaeva.

INTRODUCTION

I started work for my father as a "Saturday Boy' during the mid-1970s at his old Regent Road shop, in Salford, Manchester. I started work proper in 1979 after Dad had moved from Regent Road to the Deansgate shop, in Manchester city centre.

I'd grown up in the various sewing machine shops that my father had traded from and I was always fascinated by the whole business. I liked all the sewing machines and later I enjoyed the technical aspects of how they worked and, more importantly, how to repair them.

However, what fascinated me most was all the people that came into the shops to buy sewing machines and their various accessories.

I've now worked in the family business for more than thirty-seven years. During this time, I've met thousands of customers, and some of my encounters with them, and the people connected with the trade in general, are the reason I've written this little book of short stories.

I hope you enjoy it.

A NIGHT WITH THE STARS

My brother Steve and I attended a Bernina trade meeting a couple of years ago for the launch of three new models. The event was held at an hotel in London, not far from Euston Station. For as long as I can remember, we have made the trip down to London every year or so to visit the Bogods – the wonderful family business that distributes

Bernina sewing machines to dealers in the UK and Ireland. We always stay at the President Hotel in Russell Square where, some years ago, those with demented minds blew up a bus and carried out further acts of inhumane cruelty across London.

The trip in the car with my brother is always an enjoyable one as it raises a certain frisson of excitement – with the chance to visit the capital and meet the Bogod boys again. As Steve drove us along, my mind revisited a happy tale that my father often repeated to us, and one that was always accompanied by gales of laughter. You should understand, dear reader, that ours was a very happy childhood, with Dad constantly repeating his own stories as well as those from Messrs Dickens and Kipling, to name just a few. Let's fly across time and land, back to a trade meeting many years ago in Manchester, the centre of the universe.

It's the 1970s and a bitterly cold day in November. Winter holds the city tightly in her cruel grasp. Icy winds blow through the many corridors of the dark and snow-covered streets. Workers and shoppers are wrapped in many layers, and tears come to their eyes with the cold. The scene is the the Midland Hotel which, you may recall, was the meeting place of a certain Mr Rolls and a certain Mr Royce, who went on to enjoy some success creating a rather grand range of motor cars.

Unlike today's sewing machine trade meetings, this was a very male affair and, it being in Manchester, it attracted more than the normal share of northern dealers. I'm not sure of the geographical or cultural equivalent in America, but the 1970s northern UK dealer was usually a very tough and no-nonsense type of chap.

Let's join this group of men in the conference room as they are seated around a long table. The manufacturer's agents and distributors were in attendance (the make shall remain nameless). Most, if not all, of our group smoked, and I mean the kind of smoking which gave most of them two deeply stained dark brown patches on their fingers. My own father easily smoked eighty to a hundred Benson & Hedges king-sized cigarettes every day followed by a pipeful of St Bruno Rough Cut tobacco after most evening meals. So, the room, which was quite grand and ornate, with a high ceiling, mouldings, cornices and thick, good-quality carpets, was soon filled with a fug of thick smoke. The meeting was to launch a new product and to further discuss how to increase the sales of the brand in question. One of the top executives posed this particular question to our group. So, each man in turn offered their thoughts.

Some were good, and some were silly, and some, who considered themselves to be at least as important as the president of the mighty United States of America (there's always one – still is) would groan on and on until someone told him to put a bloody sock in it for Pete's sake. The question was finally asked of the last dealer, a short but very broad chap who sported a snugly fitting houndstooth jacket, tattersall double cuffed shirt with cufflinks, and a knitted wool tie. He had a deeply weathered face which carried a magnificent pair of 'pork-chop' sideburns, the type where even hair from the ears has joined in to assist with the overall effect. Our man took a few slow puffs from his old and worn briar pipe, blowing plumes of thick smoke across the table in a similar fashion to a newly surfaced whale as it takes its first blows. He took the pipe from his mouth and the room waited in silent anticipation.

He looked the smartly suited and booted executive dead in the eye. 'I haven't had a shit for a week.'

The room erupted with howls of laughter, sides were split, and tears ran down many cheeks. The president of the United States of America was outraged and stormed out, no doubt because the broad chap in the houndstooth had made the bigger impression. Now our man sat, stoically, puffing away on his briar with no expression upon his well-worn countenance. The meeting broke up and was called to a close.

My father found one of his chums, a dealer from the Merseyside area – let's call him Reg. The room began to clear as dealers from further afield left to catch a train or make the long journey home by car. Meanwhile, Dad and Reg decided that as it was only late afternoon, they should investigate the opportunities for a few drinks. After some wandering, they came upon a large double door at the end of a corridor. Pushing it open revealed a huge room set with many chairs and tables. At the far corner of this room was a very smart and very well-stocked bar, brightly lit and with a dark green leather frontage. Behind the bar stood a barman, waiting patiently for a customer to serve.

Dad and Reg sailed across the room in convoy, landed at the bar, and gave the barman their orders. Slowly, the room began to fill with various men and women, until the room was filled with laughter and chatter and drinking and smoking. A large side door opened and a waiter appeared to announce, 'Ladies and gentlemen, dinner is served!' The body of people slowly rose from their chairs and stools and shuffled along and into a gloriously set dining room.

There were six large dining tables and Dad and Reg took two places at one table and carried on chatting. And so they enjoyed a real Christmas feast of turkey and Christmas pud and all the trimmings washed down by a few glasses of nice champagne. Suddenly, the chink, chink, chink of a fork being tapped against a glass. A woman who had been seated at the head of another table had taken to her feet. The room fell silent. Dad thought he recognised the woman, and some of the people sat at her table seemed vaguely familiar.

The woman began to talk about how she wanted to thank

all the cast and crew for all their hard work. It then dawned on Dad and Reg that the lady was an actress called Doris Speed, and she starred in a very long-running English soap opera called *Coronation Street*. Her 'vaguely familiar' fellow diners were the assembled cast of the show. Those who were not familar to Dad and Reg, they believed to be the crew, producers and others.

Doris asked everyone to stand for the toast and Dad and Reg joined in. After taking their seats, they looked at each other and wondered what to do. After a moment or so, they stopped a passing waiter and asked for two more glasses of champagne.

DON'T LET IT KILL YOU

Thirty-five or so years ago, after some years of training, I was sent to high schools, colleges, universities and prisons to service their sewing machines. I'd go with Tony, Paul, Vincent and Fred, our mechanics at various times. Three or four times a week we used to visit these places and service up to twenty, thirty or forty machines a time. In some weeks, we'd service one hundred or more sewing machines. I had a great time with those guys, and they taught me a lot, including how to fly fish – thanks, Fred.

Slowly and surely, the guys retired or went on to start their own businesses, etc. and I ended up travelling to all the schools and colleges on my own. Our area was Greater Manchester, which took in Manchester, Salford, Bury, Bolton, Tameside, Stockport, Trafford and Rochdale. I serviced hundreds and hundreds of sewing machines, mainly Berninas and Singers with some Pfaffs, Newhomes, Janomes, Elnas and others. Most of the high schools I visited were pleasant enough, and I'd set up camp in a corner of a classroom and work away for a morning or afternoon.

The bigger schools took a full day, sometimes two. The kinder teachers ensured I got a cup of tea or coffee, and some even offered a slice of cake. Some of the schools were quite grand and parents had to pay heavily to send their children to them. Some of the schools, on the other hand, were horrible, and the staff and the students just as bad. The worst was a school where the students threw bricks at me and my van. I did the work, sent the invoice, and was paid, but they are now on my excommunicated list – a position they share with just eight other schools over a thirty-seven year period, so not too bad.

I met many 'needlework teachers', as they used to be called, and made some nice friends – even married one of them. But some were absolute horrors and walked about with permanent scowls on their faces, no doubt hating their job and their lives and making damned sure it was just as unpleasant for everyone else they met.

One teacher always sticks in my mind – we'll call her Mrs E. Mrs E worked at a small school, and most of the students were quite boisterous but generally okay. Mrs E was quite small and slight, and she never ever stopped laughing. I imagined she woke up laughing and later on drifted off to sleep chuckling to herself. She would laugh all day long, but she did have a serious side. Let any student step out of line and she could freeze them to the spot from across any classroom, admonish them fiercely, and then continue with the hilarity. I liked her a lot and we got on well. In the early days, many of the teachers I met also seemed to dress in a similar way: shampoo and set hairdo, a plain cotton or silk blouse – buttoned to the neck, thank you – teamed with a good-quality, pleated cotton skirt to the mid-calf. They wore stockings and nice plain sensible shoes for standing and walking in all day long. Jewellery was to a minimum, and if it should be worn, a plain-coloured nail varnish. Hardly any perfume, and if so, something very conservative and nothing to set any pulses racing.

The business of visiting all girls' schools was usually always embarrassing for yours truly – painfully shy, quite naive, covered in acne and a frizz of my dear mother's Irish hair. I resembled a pepperoni pizza with a Brillo Pad on top. A girl would tease and I'd go red as hell, which made the whole combo even worse. One day, driving back from a school and listening to the radio, a girl sang a sad song about learning the truth at seventeen, and I knew what she meant – but we shall move on. We started to get calls from the Merseyside area and before too long, I was flying all over Liverpool and beyond. I was always passing John Lennon's old house and almost every time there would be a group of sightseers standing about and taking photos.

Some of these schools were enormous and far bigger than any I'd seen before. One day I was booked to visit one of these larger schools and, being a stickler for timekeeping, I turned up on the dot at 9:30 a.m. as arranged. The hallway of this school for girls was very grand, and there were lots of pillars and plaster cornices and mouldings. Along one wall was a line of oak boards displaying the names, in gold, of past students and teachers of note. I presented myself at the secretary's office and was asked to wait for Miss J. A few moments later, Miss J appeared and introduced herself and we shook hands, then I followed her down a corridor. There were even more 'boards of achievement' lining the walls as we walked.

We reached Miss J's room and she opened the door and ushered me in. The room was very neat and very tidy, and there were no students in at the time. Miss J was extremely well spoken and in every respect, a lady. She was not exactly a *young* woman, but had a beautiful smile and she dressed plainly, but well. I set to work servicing the group of about twenty Berninas, mainly 801s, 807s and the odd 830. I'd remove all the covers and check the motors and the brushes and the foot controls and the leads and clean the raceways and check the belts and balance the tensions, then lubricate and test sew each one of them.

Miss J sat at her desk marking her books, back very straight, legs folded at the knee and very prim and very proper – and very quiet. A bell rang and she rose from her desk and asked if I'd care for a cup of tea, which I did. Later, when I'd finished servicing the machines, I gave my report to Miss J about the state of her Berninas and said goodbye, and just as I was leaving the room, a bell rang again and suddenly, from the many doors that lined the long corridor, out spilled hundreds and hundreds and hundreds of girls. They were shouting and screaming and singing and shoving – it was hometime. I found an empty room and ducked in to wait for the tide to ebb.

I visited Miss J again about a year later, and this time her room was full of girls. The room was in riot, and though Miss J, who was obviously at her wits end, was shouting at the girls to behave, they took no notice. I stood in the doorway and looked at her, and she at me, and I could see the pain of embarrassment in her eyes. I spent a morning in the classroom, and the girls were vile and obscene and very cruel. Finally, it was lunchtime, and the girls left Miss J and I alone, although their din seemed to ring in my ears for another five minutes or so. It was about ten minutes before Miss J came over to me, and she said she was sorry for the behaviour of her girls. I told her she had no reason to apologise.

Miss J then told me how old she was and I was surprised, because she was quite a bit older than she looked. She explained that she had worked at the school for nearly forty years, and in her time the school had gone from being a shining beacon of manners and achievement to an absolute disgrace. This had obviously had a very bad effect on her.

In visiting so many hundreds of schools over so many years, I often found that teachers would confide in me about the way they felt about the school, the staff and the students. Probably because I was an outsider and a stranger and could tell no tales in the classroom or the staffroom. Or, despite everything, maybe I had a trustworthy face.

I visited the school again a year or two later. Miss J greeted me warmly and shook my hand and seemed happy to see me. I was always happy to see her. She was, for me anyway, a lady of distinction and, well, manners maketh man and all that. Miss J warned me she would be teaching a particularly challenging class that morning, and that I should brace myself. Brace was an understatement. About half an hour in, I had been invited by two of the girls to, ahem, do whatever I liked with them. This opened the floodgates, and soon the girls were in uproar and nothing Miss J did or said made the slightest difference. She left the room, and a few moments later she returned with a male member of staff. He was a tall and chubby chap, and he bellowed at the top of his lungs for silence. The silence came, but the shock of it started the girls giggling and the giggles turned to full-blown laughter. Suddenly, one of the girls shouted out a name at the chubby teacher, which I won't repeat, and the class sank into demented chaos.

Miss J and the male teacher politely asked me to leave and I did so, all too willingly. A few years passed and one day I took a call from a lady who introduced herself as a friend of Miss J. She explained that Miss J would very much like to see me next time I was in the area, would I care to drop by her home for tea and a chat? I replied that I would be delighted to do so and I took down the address details. So, a few weeks later I straightened my tie and brushed back the frizz and knocked on Miss J's door.

It was opened by a lady who introduced herself as the one who had made the phone call. She invited me in and I stepped into a very smart house indeed. The lady showed me down the hallway and into a large sitting room. Good-quality carpets, wallpaper and curtains – all in pale green and cream pastel shades. I spotted Miss J sitting in an armchair with her back to me. The friend invited me to take a seat on a large green dralon couch, and I did so. The couch was covered in expensive cushions covered in floral embroidery. I sat and faced Miss J and noticed straight away that something wasn't quite the same about her. Her eyes were strange, and when she spoke, she did so rather slowly.

We began chatting and she explained how over the last few years the school and the behaviour of the girls had become all too much for her to bear. She had carried on at the school because of her sense of duty, but now she could carry on no longer. We drank tea from her china cups and saucers and picked biscuits from her china plates, and in a corner a clock tick-tocked and the afternoon sun picked out motes as they sailed across the room. She continued and explained that she had suffered a serious nervous breakdown and was under the care of a doctor and on strong medication.

Her friend, sitting on another armchair, gave me a slight nod and a smile.

I stayed for more than two hours, and we chatted and had the odd small laugh, and then Miss J looked tired and it was time for me to go. I shook Miss J's hand and she placed a gentle kiss on my cheek and we wished each other well, and then the friend showed me to the door and thanked me for coming.

I never saw Miss J again and never went back to the school. These days, I sit in my office and I don't go out to schools any more like I once did. I do travel all over the UK helping people set up their embroidery businesses with the Brother PR655. I work on our online presence and our mail order catalogues etc. I organise our mechanics – Shahid and Luke – to call and collect machines from schools to be serviced in our workshop, and I speak to many teachers on the phone and lots of them come into our store for a chat.

Sometimes they tell me about the problems they face at school and I always tell them – 'Don't let it kill you'.

FISHING FOR WRASSE

I've always enjoyed fishing. Have done ever since I was a boy. One day, my father bought me a fishing kit from Woolworths. Rod, reel, line etc., you know the kind of thing. Or maybe you don't. That was the sixties, and kids these days seem to prefer a virtual world where nothing is real – except for the cost.

My rod was green with metal ferrules, and I fished any piece of water I found on our early caravan holidays in Devon and Cornwall – but not Manchester. Her rivers ran thick with poison and all that dwelt within their greasy depths was sickness and death. These days, fly fishing is my thing, and every now and then I like to escape the phone calls, the emails and the general pull of it all. My favourite time of year is the autumn, or fall, as some might say; when the summer has headed off somewhere far beyond the curve and now the dawn air delivers only a crisp chill to the early riser. Those are the days when I like to find myself waist-deep in a river and be surrounded only by trees and fields and sky.

The best of times are those when midday might bring an hour of sun to warm the face and back and I might catch half a glimpse of gold and turquoise as a kingfisher darts low and fast along a riverbank. And, if I'm very lucky, a plump trout might take my fly and take some line and bend my rod. They all go back – just a few moments so I can marvel at their beauty, but they all go back. All too soon the sun slips away and the chill returns and it's time for me to leave my paradise. Home again, I'll enjoy a small whisky and sit and quietly remember my day and all the wonders that came my way. A hot meal with my wife and a prayer of thanks and then to bed.

A few years back, I got a taste for the sea and set off for the coast in search of wrasse. My favourite spot was Trearddur Bay on Holy Island just off Anglesey. I'd climb down the rocks and walk along the coast, leaving all the daytrippers behind me. Then I'd cast my rod and wait and wait for the pluck, pluck pluck of a wrasse. One day I'd gone a fair old way to find some peace. When finally I did, I cast my rod and began to wait. The sun was high in a bright blue sky and a strong salty breeze slowly turned my cheeks to red. The sea swelled and rolled and sea birds wheeled and climbed and cried and all was well in my own small world.

It was only then that I noticed someone else standing a little way off from where I stood. An older chap, an old timer, standing there, like me – fishing. He spotted me looking and I looked away, but I looked again to see he wore an old green mac belted at the waist and green over-trousers – waterproofs. I nodded and he lifted his chin maybe an inch and then he looked away and carried on fishing.

The wrasse weren't biting so I reeled in and fixed my line. I looked again at the old timer and walked over towards him as he watched me.

'No luck today,' I said.

'Nor for me,' he replied.

Silence.

'I'm Alan,' I said, and offered him my hand.

He returned the favour and said his name was John. He was old, his beard was grey and his skin was brown and lined with age – and the sea, perhaps. In my rucksack, I carried a flask and some sandwiches wrapped in brown paper and I knelt and pulled them both from the bag.

'I've got sandwiches and some coffee, if you fancy some,' I said.

He sat and I poured him a coffee, but he wouldn't eat; instead, he pulled a pipe from his pocket and stuffed it with tobacco. He leant away from the breeze and lit the pipe with a long match from an old silver box. I poured another coffee and unwrapped my sandwiches and we sat together and watched the sea.

After a while, John pulled a small bottle of brandy from another pocket and emptied some of it into his coffee. He held up the bottle and looked at me, and I nodded back at him. He poured a small shot into my coffee, and I took a sip and felt the warmth as the spirit warmed my own. We began to talk. John had been a sailor, in war and peace. He'd sailed on the Russian convoys, like one of my uncles, to Murmansk and Archangel. Now he was old and his wife had passed and his children grown – so he liked to fish and look at the sea and to be quiet and think his thoughts alone.

He asked me what I did.

'Sewing machines,' I said.

'My wife loved to sew,' he replied. 'Bought her a fancy machine from a store in Manchester. A Bernini or something.'

'Bamber's?' I asked.

'That's the one!'

I had another sandwich and watched the sea.

FIVE BAR GATE

Some years ago, I took a phone call from a lady. She told me her Bernina was playing up and could we come out and collect it. She also told me she was wheelchair-bound and rarely left the house. I told her I would. She thanked me and passed me on to her husband for directions.

Despite Manchester once being one of the main industrial workshops of the world and, of course, being the very centre of the universe, we are surrounded by some beautiful countryside. And so the chap explained he was a farmer and he and his good lady wife lived on their farm some twenty-odd miles away. A date and time was agreed, and come the day, I set off to collect the Bernina.

When I'd spoken to the farmer, he'd explained how to find his farm, which was to be found down various country lanes and tracks – turn left at the telephone box, on to the small bridge over the river, turn left when you see the old oak, and so on . . . He'd also told me that as I drove along the track through his land, I'd come to a five bar gate, and it was more than likely there would be a horse on the other side. The horse, it seemed, despite having acre upon acre to roam across, always chose to stand just on the other side of this gate – and just close enough so you couldn't open the gate to drive through. The farmer had instructed me that on reaching the five bar gate with the horse on the other side, to get out of my vehicle and climb the gate and push the horse out of the way.

'He's a friendly sort, just daft as a brush, and he won't kick or bite,' the farmer had said.

I found the farm, eventually, and drove along the track until I reached the five bar gate. Up in the distance, I could see the farmhouse sitting on top of a hill. Meanwhile, I'd alighted from the van and was looking at a horse that was looking at me. The horse had his rather fat rear end up against the gate and was chewing some grass, looking at me over his shoulder in a very uninterested manner.

He dropped one hip as if to firm up his position and fix himself to the spot as I climbed the gate. He swung his head to see what I was up to, and I don't mind confessing that I was a little uneasy about how things might turn out. You see, I don't spend much of my time pushing horses around fields – *you* might be an Olympic champion at it, but not me. The horse watched me as I gingerly moved forward and placed both my hands on his rump. I made damned sure I was not in his kicking line – *damned sure*. I pushed, and the horse didn't move. I pushed again. Still no movement.

The sun was climbing to its zenith, and all I could hear was the horse, munching the grass, and a kind of a low buzzing sound coming from the land. I took off my overall and threw it over the gate. I pushed again, only harder, and again, and again, and then I leaned into it and I began to shove – to no effect. The horse just kind of leaned back into me and didn't budge an inch, all the while carrying on eating the grass. I looked up at the farm, and for a moment I wondered if the farmer and wife were staring down at me and laughing their socks off. Maybe it was a regular thing they did for amusement and the horse was in on it.

I took a step away from the horse and took a breather, and the horse lowered his head and munched the grass. I rolled up my sleeves and prepared for an almighty push and shove, and thought to use my shoulder and back and everything else. The horse carried on munching away, entirely unconcerned. I began to talk to the horse and explain my predicament, and how I needed to collect his mistress's sewing machine. He paid me no attention, so I stroked his back and gave him a nice scratch and his flanks began to quiver, but still he stood there.

Suddenly, a flash of inspiration. On the other side of the gate, along the sides of the track, the grass was quite green and lush. I climbed the gate to the other side and pulled out two great handfuls of the grass, and then I climbed back over to the horse. I walked past him with the grass in my hand and I brushed a handful under his nose, and what do you know? He trotted over, and I backed away, and he trotted more, and I backed away further.

I left the grass on the ground for him to munch and ran

back to the five bar gate, opened it and drove through. I shut the gate and drove past the horse and up to the farmhouse and as I passed, I'm sure that horse winked at me . . .

GIRLS AND THEIR MOTHERS

One day, I slipped out of the store to deliver a mighty Bernina 790E to a lady just a few miles down the road. After twenty minutes or so, I arrived at the lady's place of work – it was one of those mirrored glass and steel office blocks with a grumpy man operating the electric doors. I'm sure you know the kind of place I'm talking about.

I pushed a door but to no avail – it was locked. So, carrying the bulky box containing the embroidery unit, I walked over to a revolving door. It sailed away as soon as it detected me, so the box and I took our chances and jumped in, hoping for the best. It was quite a squeeze, and the doors didn't slow down as they shoved us along and then threw us both out inside the building.

'I saw you struggling with that box,' the grumpy man said. After that, he was a bit stumped for further conversation, so I mentioned the lady's name and he pressed a button. I imagined that somewhere in the building a light flashed on someone's desk and they knew that this was the sign to leave their work and report to reception.

A delightful lady appeared with a lovely smile; she shook my hand and showed me outside to her car. The grumpy man managed to open the door for us, and he tried to smile but he didn't quite manage it, so he went back to looking grumpy – and it kind of suited him.

I heaved the 790 and the embroidery unit into the nice lady's car and she began to talk. She told me that this was her sixth sewing machine, and maybe her last as she was retiring from work this Christmas. She told how her mother had bought her a sewing machine when she was a girl, and that her mother had taught her how to sew. Through the years, the lady had visited our store – she remembered my father – and bought other machines, and she'd bought a

Bernina and loved it, but now she'd given it to her own daughter.

Then, she told me that her mother had died and how she'd left her some money, and she'd used some of that money to buy the mighty Bernina 790E. I told her to call in to our store for all the tuition and help she needed, and she thanked me and said that she would.

And then she held out her hand for me to shake, which I did, although what I really wanted to do was to put my arms around her, hold on to her for a while and give her a kiss on her cheek – maybe both – and tell her how much I loved her.

And that is me – I love all you Bernina Girls.

LULLABY ON A WET AFTERNOON

It's raining as I write this, and it reminds me one of my favourite calls: an adult education college in Manchester. They had about twenty sewing machines – mainly Berninas and Pfaffs and all very well used – and I'd usually have to spend a full morning or afternoon completing all the work.

Over the years, different teachers came and went, and most were nice and some were not, but that's people for you. The local ladies who made up the class were almost all from Jamaica or the West Indies, and they produced some fabulous work and lots of nice outfits and lovely hats. At the end of each year they would have a fashion show to show off what they had made, and then they would pin all the photographs of the show on the classroom wall.

Visiting this college was always a very welcome change from the many high schools I visited as some of the students could be extremely loud and unpleasant. On some days, when it was pouring with rain, I might have visited a high school in the morning, serviced all their machines, and then travelled on to a college in the afternoon. And on a wet afternoon it was nice to slowly dry off as I serviced the machines in such a peaceful and warm classroom.

It was one of those old-fashioned Manchester high school buildings. Outside there was a door for the girls and a door for the boys. Inside, all the brick walls were painted a very shiny brown and the huge windows were very high up so the original children could not be distracted by looking outside. Also, the heating system was similar to something you would find in the Queen Mary, and when the heating was on it was like being in the tropics.

Sometimes I would be sitting quietly in a corner of the classroom working on the machines and the ladies would be sitting about the room sewing up their creations and chatting away to each other, and every now and then they'd say hello to me. Suddenly, one of the ladies would begin to sing very softly, or just hum a gentle tune. Then another lady would join in, and before you knew where you were, the entire class would be singing and harmonising, and those songs seemed to reach inside you and, just for a few moments, cradle your soul and make you feel very happy indeed.

As time went by, I started to visit some of these ladies in their homes to service their own sewing machines, and I got to know them and they got to know me. Everything was lovely.

MAC THE KNIFE

Before we moved to the store we're in now, we had one on Oldham Street, in Manchester's city centre. We were there for almost twenty years. When we first moved to Oldham Street in the early 1980s, the area was quite neglected and had remained largely untouched for the last fifty years – or more. The developers had not yet begun to turn the old nearby mill buildings into trendy and expensive apartments for trendy and expensive people.

Our store was on the corner of Oldham Street and Stephenson Square, and at the top of Oldham Street, some few hundred yards away, was an area called Ancoats, where the old mills and large tenement buildings stood. Behind the tenement buildings was an old and overgrown and unused park. In the early days, we had to park our vehicles down the side streets along the tenements and the park, and this was also the home of the city's many tramps. On warm summer mornings I'd often see a long line of these guys snoozing away and sleeping off yesterday's intake of methylated spirits and cheap liquor, and I have to confess that once or twice I slipped one or two of them a few quid to help them find their chosen oblivion.

As the morning wore on, these guys would gradually wake, stretch, retch and gradually wander off through their chosen corridors of the city beyond. Oldham Street was also home to many old-fashioned and very traditional pubs – large and small. And facing our store was the epicentre of drinking establishments for the seasoned and dedicated alcoholic. It was a small place with just some basic bench seating, a few tables and chairs and a small stage with a standing microphone. Each lunchtime would see a small and shuffling crowd gather outside the pub. Watches would be checked and windows would be peered through and the closer it got to opening time, the more fidgety and restless the small crowd became until finally the landlord, unshaven, unkempt and fag in mouth, would 'open up'.

I imagined at the time that the same bar and the same crowd and the same landlord existed in other parts of the world, such as New York or Boston. The clientele were largely men, and they more or less all adhered to a general dress code of cheap and poorly fitted suits teamed with a plain white or blue shirt. Some sported several of those sovereign-type rings you used to see. Classy. Those that didn't would have each finger tattooed with the obligatory 'LOVE' and 'HATE'. If they were a serious style icon, they would have both. A number of them also used about a quarter of a pound of Brylcreem so they could comb back their hair – a slight quiff on top and straight back and down behind. They always carried a comb, usually in the top pocket of their suit jackets, and every twenty minutes or so they'd pull out the comb, drop their heads but still keep eye contact, and comb everything back in place while smoothing it all down with their other hand.

The party piece was to do all this while talking to their compadre and smoking a fag. You just can't find that kind of style amongst the pages of *Cosmopolitan*, or *Conde Nast* or the swankier bars of Manhattan's Upper East Side anymore. But then standards have slipped so much these days . . .

The women who patronised the place were usually the old bar and nightclub singers or similar, and they wore sparkly dresses – a bit too short and a bit too low and a bit too tight – teamed with corned-beef legs or fishnet stockings. As each day wore on, the men would swap 'hot tips' on dogs, and horses and – forgive me – women, and some of these would be noted down as 'sure-fire-bets' and be accompanied by a wink of the eye, a quick comb of the hair and a flash of the sovereign rings.

The women, meanwhile, would swap tales of nightclubs and bars and men and beatings. Once in a while, I'd enjoy a quick lunchtime pint in their company, and I counted myself as no better and no worse than any of them for we are all God's children, and who amongst us should judge the other?

At any given point during their hours of intoxication, any one of the assembled cast was likely to take to the stage and offer up a song for the benefit of all. Usually, the song told of love or lost chances – or both – and predictably Mr Sinatra's 'My Way' featured heavily. Sometimes a shoe or ashtray would fly across the room and strike the crooner and cause much merriment and shouting and swearing. Sometimes a song would strike a chord, and a woman sitting alone in a corner, nursing a port and lemon, would shed a tear onto her cheek remembering a lost youth or love – or both.

Late afternoon in high summer was the time for fights to break out – the heat, the drink, the baloney. Of course, fighting was strictly forbidden in the pub by order of the landlord, and guilty parties were banned for twelve months. And so, when the talk of dogs and horses and women met with too much disagreement, everyone would stagger outside, blinking in the sunshine, and the fight would ensue on the street. This usually coincided with someone in our store trying to demonstrate a Bernina, or Elna, or Pfaff to a smart and well-dressed, fragrant lady. Afterwards, the winner and the loser and their audience would stagger back into the pub, several of the men would take the opportunity to pull out their combs and, well, you know the story by now . . . Drinking would resume inside; it was a serious business.

One day, I saw a man take a beating from his wife, or girlfriend, or acquaintance – who was in a wheelchair. He stood obediently still as she swung at him with her large black handbag. Each blow was accompanied by a curse, and she timed blow and curse quite well – as if she'd done it before. Thoughtfully, she informed him when the beating was at an end and his punishment was over, and he then dutifully and gently wheeled her back inside. The small crowd shuffled in behind them.

Another day, two men walked into our store – one casually dressed and one in a smart three-piece pinstriped suit. We had many sewing machines on show, and one of our sales girls, Alison, now a very close family friend, let out a shout as she spotted the men trying to steal an Elna TSP. What a swine. I was in the workshop at the back of the store and I heard Alison scream, 'They're stealing a machine!'

I gave chase, being somewhat younger, dafter, slimmer and fleeter of foot than I am these days. Outside on the street, the casually dressed man had disappeared, but I spotted the pinstriped thief and he spotted me. He broke into a run and I began to chase after him – and I began gaining on him. He was older and chubbier than me, and he was running out of puff. The gap between us shortened, when suddenly he stopped, turned and reached inside his jacket.

He pulled out a large and cruel-looking knife. Looking at the weasel, I could see that he didn't have the Elna about him. So, after giving him the benefit of my thoughts on the matter, I departed the scene, intact but cursing my luck, for surely I had chased the wrong thief and the casually dressed guy had made off with our Elna. I was quite downhearted; it was personal, after all.

All turned out well, though, because when I returned to the store, Alison had found the Elna. The two swines had dropped it on a corner as they fled the scene. We moved from Oldham Street to our present store around eleven or twelve years ago when the local council changed a bus route. This meant we could no longer park outside the store and, more importantly, neither could our customers.

This 'new' store is in a much quieter and safer area and our customers like it, but I often cast a glance to the street outside and wonder where all the 'action' went.

MRS Z

I first met Mrs Z in the early 1980s. She was the needlework teacher at a large and boisterous co-ed school in Lancashire. Walking down a corridor during a visit one day, I opened a door for her. That small courtesy seemed to mean a lot, and it was reported back to my father. She was German, about five feet tall in her heels and she smoked Cafe Creme cigars. Her very deep and loud German voice could be heard at the furthest corner of even the longest corridor. And I'm pretty sure that the whole school – kids, staff, head teacher and even the PE teacher – were absolutely terrified of her.

Despite her diminutive size, even the tallest and roughest of boys would stand aside as she marched imperiously through the school.

'Alahn, vonderful to see you again,' she'd say, and then, 'How is your fahrter?'

This, of course, always caused much merriment, and even she would chuckle, which sounded a bit like the gurgling and choking sound a toilet makes after it's been flushed and starts to refill. Mrs Z had a soft spot for my father, possibly because he was the only man she knew who could out-smoke her.

She always wore a very smart Chanel or Christian Dior-style suit and heavy brogues, the type with a strap and a thick two-inch cutaway, or Cuban heel. Also her stockings – I imagine they were silk, and they were usually the colour of Bisto gravy. She was . . . magnificent.

In those days, we used to collect the sewing machines from dozens of schools at the end of every July so we could service and repair them over the summer holidays. The teachers, meanwhile, would be sunning themselves in Torremolinos, or Bognor, or at home on the gin and Mogadon. In Mrs Z's case, it was St Tropez, I imagined.

One day, at work, I was handed the telephone. My father took all the calls as I was considered too young to answer a telephone call from a customer. The phone call was from Mrs Z and she explained that she was leaving well before the end of term to visit her sick mother in Germany, and would I mind collecting her sewing machines in her absence, as usual? I said I would and hung up feeling quite sad that I wouldn't see her until the new term began in September.

So it was that I arrived at the school one day in late July about thirty-odd years ago. Term had ended and, as ever, there wasn't a soul to be seen. I eventually found a cleaner polishing the parquet in the assembly hall. I explained I'd called to collect the sewing machines and was duly given directions to the staff room, where I was assured I'd find the caretaker and his team. I knocked and then pushed open the door to the staff room and there before me were around seven or eight men sprawled over pushed-together chairs and tables – one chap was completely fast asleep. The rest were puffing away on fags, reading newspapers and drinking tea. Jimmy Young was waffling away on the radio.

I spotted the oldest-looking of the group and explained I'd called to collect the sewing machines, all forty or so of them, for repair and service. One of the younger element advised me to 'eff-off' and a few of the others encouraged me to do the same. The older chap suggested I call back in September; they were all too busy and it would be better when the school reopened 'for that kind of thing, son'.

They all returned to puffing away, reading papers and slurping their tea.

'Okay,' I said. 'I'll call back in September. But would you mind informing Mrs Z that I called as arranged and you sent me away?'

A sounder of slumbering warthogs warming themselves in the late afternoon sun and then catching sight of a hungry lion could not have jumped to their trotters quicker than the caretaker and his team at the mention of Mrs Z's name. A fight almost broke out about who had the keys, and I was soon chasing after the group as we raced down stairs, round corners, up stairs – why are there always so many bloody stairs? – and along corridors to reach Mrs Z's room in record time. There was soon a chain of men, stretching from the needlework classroom to my van outside, each man handing the other a sewing machine.

I left with the caretaker's best wishes and his best to Mrs Z.

OLD MEN

L et's journey back to a time many moons ago when the mighty Bernina 830 was a new and current model.

A chap walked in off the street and into my father's store and he asked to be shown the very best sewing machine on sale. The man explained he wished to buy a birthday present for his dear lady wife. My father led the chap over to the 830 and began to proudly explain its merits. The man cut Dad short, pulled out his chequebook and asked, 'How much is it and can you deliver one to my address at 3 p.m. next Thursday?' His wife would then be out of the house paying a visit to her mother.

Dad did as he was bade and dutifully delivered the 830. The months and years slipped by, and the chap popped in every so often to buy an extra foot or attachment when a birthday or Christmas arrived. One year he even bought a rather smart cabinet for his wife's machine. He and his wife, he told my father, now had a family, and his wife made all the clothes for their two young girls on the 830.

A few years ago, the chap appeared once more, now an old and quite frail man. He remembered my father, who was semi-retired himself by then. They spoke, as old men do, about old times and when they were young and how they once bestrode the world with vigour and love as if to remind each other that those golden days were real, and not just some hazy half-forgotten dream. The man went on to explain how time had stolen his wife's once sharp faculties, and she now spent her days in an old folks' home. She could no longer sew.

The chap asked my father to call and collect the still mighty Bernina 830, the cabinet and all the attachments she'd bought over those years. My father asked the chap how much he wanted in return.

'Not one penny,' replied the man. That Bernina, he

explained, had clothed his family and given his wife so much pleasure over so many years. His only request was that the 830 should go to a good home.

They shook hands and the chap departed. A few days later, we collected the 830 and the cabinet and we placed it in our store for sale. Not long after, a very smart lady and her daughter walked into our store and were both very taken by the 830. I explained the merits of it to the lady, who could have easily afforded any machine in our store.

The daughter, a college fashion student, had previously used the Bernina 830 in her classes and, having seen our 830 sat snugly in the cabinet, looked as though she had just fallen deeply in love. The mother presented her credit card and the sale was made.

I like to think the daughter will find someone decent, kind and caring, and the story will begin all over again.

GIRL IN BLACK

B ack in the early eighties, I was beavering away in the workshop of our Oldham Street store when one of our sales girls popped her head round the corner and asked me to come and help a customer. So I put my tools down and wiped my hands – wouldn't wish to present myself to a customer with dirty hands.

Hands clean, I walked into the store and saw a young woman standing at the counter. I'd say she was in her early twenties, about the same age as myself at the time. She was dressed head to toe in black and she was what I believe they call a 'Goth'. She wore a black corset – laced at the front, a rather tight and short black skirt, and black stockings of the type which, after I explained them to my wife, I've learned are called hold-ups. Anyway, these hold-ups were holding up just below the hemline of her skirt, and they were laddered – on both legs. She also wore a pair of Doc Marten boots, unlaced, and, you guessed it, black. A heavy black leather motorcycle jacket, sporting pointed silver studs arching across both shoulders, finished the ensemble.

Her long black hair was as black as black ink; it was so black it almost looked blue in places, like the breast of a blackbird spotted in the snowy winter's garden. Her face was powdery white and pale and she wore an awful lot of black eye shadow. She had quite full lips – deep purple. I mean really deep purple, almost black.

I asked the girl how I could help her. She placed both her hands on the glass-topped counter and I noticed that her long nails were jet black, and she noticed that I noticed and started to tap those nails on the glass, as the panther might when extending the claws just before leaping for the throat. She tilted her head to one side and, moving only her eyes, looked me up and down. She didn't seem impressed with what she saw – not that she should have been, you understand.

'My sewing machine is broken,' she said, finally. 'I need someone to fix it.'

'Well,' I replied, 'if you would bring your machine into our store, I'll take a look at it and see what can be done—'

'I can't bring it in,' she interrupted. 'And I don't drive, and anyway it's too heavy. I don't have much money either.' She looked me straight in the eye as she delivered this last line with quite the defiant look on her powdery white face. Daring me, it seemed, to challenge her in some way. The nails tapped again.

I mulled things over for a moment and then I asked the girl where she lived. When she told me where, I knew that I passed her home all the time when out visiting schools to service their machines. She lived in one of the many council-owned high-rise flats that used to climb into the grey skies of central Manchester. They all met their demise some years back when riots and bombs persuaded the government of the time to dig deep into the public purse and redevelop. They have been largely replaced now by private snazzy apartment blocks which climb into Manchester's still grey skies.

I asked the girl's name and address and she told me her name was Miss Ritz – it was something else but you'll forgive me if courtesy prevails and I keep that to myself, dear reader. I took out my diary and pencilled in a date that suited us both. I looked up from the page and met her gaze and her eyes narrowed.

'Don't let me down,' she said, and she turned on her Doc-Martened heel and loped out into the bustle of Oldham Street and was gone.

A few days later, I was driving back from a local city centre school after servicing numerous machines. I pulled off the busy street and into the small courtyard at the foot of the high-rise flats. Carrying the toolbox my father had shown me how to make – dovetail joints and all – I walked to the entrance and cast an eye up the sheer cliff wall of the high rise. The block looked like something from 1950s communist Moscow – or at least that's how I imagined things looked in 1950s communist Moscow. In any event, I pitied the poor blighters condemned to live in such a place.

It was a freezing cold day and it had just begun to rain. Inside, the dark concrete floors and walls of the hallway were wet and there was an unpleasant pong of urine. Inevitably, the girl lived on almost the top floor and, inevitably, as I walked over to the two lifts/elevators, I spotted the 'Out of Order' signs stuck to the doors. I took to the stairs and began my ascent.

Finally, I reached the floor where the girl lived and walked along an open balcony as I counted down the numbers to her door. The wind was biting, and the rain was slanted at forty-five degrees; it cut into my face and soaked me. I found the number I was looking for and knocked on the door, and after a moment, it opened, but only so far. A chain snapped the door to a stop with a gap of around five or six inches. I recognised the darkly shadowed eye staring out from the gloom. The wind was beginning to make small howling noises, and I was beginning to shiver standing there on the doorstep with my toolbox.

The door slammed shut and I heard the chain being slipped from its anchor. The door opened fully this time and there stood the girl in her doorway.

'Hello, I've come like I promised to see what can be done with your machine,' I said.

She just stood there, holding her door ajar, staring at me. It was clear she still didn't trust me, and it was a little bit tense and a little bit awkward. I thought she might slam the door shut and that would be that.

'You'd better come in,' she said, finally.

So I took a step into her lair and wondered what I might find. There was something of the witch about this young woman. Or so I thought. She showed me along a small hallway and into a small and unremarkable living room heated by a three-bar electric fire.

'Would you mind if I warm myself by your fire?' I asked.

She shook her head slightly and said no. I took a few paces over to the fire and felt a shiver as the heat embraced me. She was dressed in a similar way to the first time we met – a black leather dress with two straps over her bare pale shoulders and her arms were also bare and milk white. She was also wearing the same kind of hold-ups and boots. She reached for a black sweater from the settee and pulled it on quickly, dragging her long hair out from underneath.

The room was poorly furnished. The carpet was bland and worn, and along one wall sat a small settee – there was no coffee or dining table. There was a clothes rack, the type you will find in any ladies' department store, holding the girl's wardrobe of various black outfits of lace and leather and PVC and denim. All hanging neatly and each, it struck me, like a uniform to be worn for a certain operation, or day or event.

I spotted her sewing machine sitting on the floor. It was a Japanese Newhome, a flatbed in a wooden base. A good machine – basic and simple and heavy, a good workhorse. The girl stood in the doorway to the room, hiding her body behind the door frame, obviously still unsure about this interruption and intrusion into her life. Only her face seemed visible, and it seemed to float in the darkness. I asked if I could take a look at her machine and she said that I could, so I got on my knees and turned the balance wheel. She took a small step or two towards me, as if she needed to be ready to protect and defend her machine. Maybe I would feel her cold claws tighten around my neck . . .

As I turned the wheel, the machine locked and wouldn't move. 'Have you got any spare newspaper? I asked.

'What for?'

'I want to lay some on the floor so I don't get any oil or dirt on your carpet,' I replied.

The girl disappeared into another room and I heard a cupboard drawer slide open. She returned with a newspaper, and she handed it to me. I took it and opened it, laying it on the floor and spreading the pages. I opened my toolbox and found a couple of my faithful screwdrivers, with well-worn handles, and I tipped the machine back and loosened the two grub screws that gripped the hinges and lifted the head from the base, sitting it on the paper. I removed the top cover and opened the side or faceplate, removed the bobbin case, slipped away the guard ring and pulled the shuttle from the raceway.

Now the machine was uncovered and I could see what was going on. I removed the needle and replaced it with a new one. After a little while and some turning of the balance wheel, backwards and forwards, I could see that the needlebar height and the shuttle timing needed adjustment, as did the feed dogs. So, I made the adjustments and I cleaned the raceway and added a drop of oil. I added further drops of oil here and there. I took a small piece of emery paper from a drawer in my toolbox and I smoothed away a few small marks from the point of the shuttle where the needle had struck it. After stripping the tension unit and cleaning the discs, I rebuilt it and tested the torsion of the check spring. I made a small adjustment to the bobbin case tension and then, finally, I did a sew test. The machine sewed like a dream and flew. A lot of the old, heavy Japanese sewing machines, like this Newhome, always seemed to sew at a hundred miles an hour – they were very fast.

The girl had moved from the door like a shadow and was now standing over me, watching. I rose to my feet. 'Your machine is fine now,' I said. I moved away and started to pack my tools back into my case. 'Try it for yourself.'

The girl lowered herself to the floor to try her machine. I thought it best not to ask why she didn't buy a small table to sit her machine on. She sat cross-legged and operated the foot control with her knee. She tested her machine, and I could see she knew how to use it – and I liked that. I often say to customers who have minor troubles with their machines that part of the secret is to try to get the 'feel' of their sewing machine. This girl in black had learned that secret. She rose and went to her clothes rack and pulled out a box from under her outfits. After a quick search, she pulled out a piece of black leather. Walking back to her machine, she gave me a look. One of her eyebrows was arched and she raised her chin slightly, as if to say *now I will test my machine my way – and you.* She placed the leather under the presser foot and began to sew. The machine sewed it perfectly, and she stopped and inspected the stitch. She sewed some more and then stopped. The girl removed the leather and cut the thread and she rose to her feet. She looked at the stitching very carefully and she looked at me and I could see she wanted to say something but couldn't find the words.

'I bet your machine has never sewed as well as that before!' I said, and handed her a packet of Leatherpoint needles I'd taken from my toolbox. 'You should use these on your leather outfits. They've got a chisel end, not a point like a regular needle, and they'll cut through the leather that bit easier.'

She reached out and took them. Then, a look of guilt – the first sign of vulnerability I'd seen from the girl in black. 'I haven't got any money to pay you,' she said.

I could have got angry, but I didn't because I'd expected as much, and anyway, I've always been a steady player.

'Don't worry,' I said. 'There's no charge.'

A look of suspicion flashed across her face now. I think she may have expected some retaliation to her response of no cash, but my reply seemed to catch her off guard. I picked up my toolbox and made for the door.

'Good luck with your outfits,' I said, and started down the hallway.

The girl, realising I truly didn't want anything from her, slipped by me and reached her front door. She turned and reached out her hand to shake mine. 'Thanks,' she said.

'You're very welcome, dear sausage,' I replied, and suddenly the girl in black with the blue/black hair and the powdery white face with purple lips gave me the most beatific smile. I found myself holding on to her hand longer than I should, but I couldn't help but linger in the warmth of that smile for a while – and she didn't seem to mind. Then I was outside, and now the wind was really howling around the damp old corridors of that high-rise block; it was still raining and my face was soon soaked, again. But somehow, I didn't seem to notice or care.

A few weeks later, I was in the store again. The doors opened and in walked a poorly dressed woman. She looked old and worn out, and her hair was unkempt and unwashed. Her face was wrinkled and weathered and dry, and her eyes were cruel and glittered with anger. Her chin was long and pointed, and two or three white hairs curled away from the point. She'd lost most of her teeth, which had caused her face to sink and only exaggerated her long pointed chin. Her bare legs were sharp and flaky, and she wore very worn flat shoes.

'You Alan?' she asked.

'Yes I am,' I replied.

'You fixed the girl's sewing machine at a few weeks ago at the high-rise flats.'

'I did.'

It seemed some kind of victory for the woman, and she sort of sneered at me.

'You mean Miss Ritz?'

A cackle of a laugh erupted from the toothless mouth. 'Miss Ritz my eye!' spat the woman. 'Jones is her name. Jones. I should know– I'm her mother.'

Another look of defiance and, looking at her, I wondered if she'd ever known love – or ever shown it. Had she ever caressed the face of the girl in black and said 'I love you, daughter of mine'?

'Anyway,' said the woman, breaking my thoughts, 'she wants some more of those leather-type needles.'

I pulled a packet from the wooden dispenser my father

had made years before. I placed them on the counter and told her the price. From one of her pockets, she pulled out a small and very worn red purse which had started to turn dark grey in places. She fingered through her change and then, finding the correct amount, slapped it down on the counter, hard, and gave me another challenging look. I thought she must go from day to day looking for conflict and disagreement.

'Thank you very much,' I said.

The woman had rocked forward a little, like she was ready for me to react in a way which would give her an excuse to attack. She pulled back, somewhat deflated that I hadn't. Her fingers scrabbled on the counter to pick up the packet of needles and she gave me one last sneer and was gone. I watched her walk down Oldham Street, a hunched figure of spite and disappointment.

Later that night I reflected, as I so often do, on the day and the days which had led up to it. Perhaps the girl in black with the white powdered face wasn't the witch – perhaps, in fact, she was an angel. May be her mother was the . . . well, I'll leave that for you to decide.

HOLE IN THE WALL GANG

W hen I was a small boy back in the early to mid-1960s, we lived in the rooms behind and above our sewing machine shop in Cadishead, Salford. Across the road, the old steelworks used to belch out thick black smoke and other noxious fumes, and the stink of it was thick in your nose and mouth.

Dad was always working so hard trying to build up his business, and me dear old mum worked even harder looking after me and Dad and then 'our kid' arrived on the scene in March '66.

Dad decided he needed a bigger shop, so one morning at around 6 a.m. he shook me awake and said, 'Come on, Alan! We're going to knock a wall down.'

Dad was – and remains – my absolute hero, so I jumped to it and chased after him.

We went downstairs and began to knock the wall down that separated the back of the shop and our tiny living room. Dad gave it hell with a short-handled lump hammer, and I cleared the bricks after they'd fallen to the floor which, you'll appreciate, was a vital role.

My pyjamas and slippers provided all the safety gear a Salford lad of four or five required. Health and safety had yet to be invented, and Dad was a tough guy and expected no less from either me, and later, my brother Steve.

Before midmorning, Dad had demolished the wall and we were both wheelbarrowing and carrying the bricks and mortar outside and into the back yard.

So, we lost our living room, much to Mum's chagrin, and for the next few years we lived in the kitchen and the two upstairs bedrooms. But Dad got his wish and the shop was now bigger.

There were a couple of parks nearby where Mum would take me to play, pushing Steve in his pram for some fresher air. One of the parks had a small concrete paddling pool which was very popular with the local kids and their mothers. You just had to be careful as the bigger kids liked to smash bottles in the dark depths of the pool so the unsuspecting paddler would cut their feet on a jagged edge.

This happened to Steve one day; there was much blood, and I seem to remember Mum using her scarf to wrap poor Stevie's lacerated foot.

My favourite park, though, was the George Thomas recreation ground, and amongst its attractions was an old decommissioned railway engine. I would pester Mum to take me there during the summer months so I could play on the engine for as long as Mum could bear it.

I'd start off somewhere in London and we'd make our way through towns and countryside and on to Scotland, watching the scenery speed by as I stood on the footplate playing both engine driver and fireman.

Happy days!

So, I grew up, in that shop and others, surrounded by women. They either loved to sew – or needed to. Those who enjoyed it might buy an expensive Bernina 730 or similar. Those who needed to, to clothe themselves and their family, bought something cheaper.

They would all ruffle my hair and maybe give me a few bob for sweets and tell me how I looked like my mother and now I am, just like father before, a sewing machine man.

ALL AT SEA

I took a call from an old friend – a needlework teacher I'd
known for a number of years. She'd left her previous
school because the head had decided to drop the subject and
had 'disposed' of all the schools' sewing machines during the
summer holidays – without her.

The teacher had returned to find all her precious Berninas
had disappeared – and her job with it . . . Several hundred
pounds' worth of Berninas had been thrown onto a rubbish
skip and dumped.

She reported that she'd now taken a job at a school on the Isle of Man and would I call and service the sewing machines? I said I would and we made a date.

I arrived at the ferry port in Liverpool and spotted the Isle of Man ferry bobbing up and down in the harbour like a bath-time toy next to the mighty Irish ferries, which were enormous by comparison. Once tickets and vehicles had been checked, the small queue of cars chugged across a gangplank and into the belly of the ferry, and we were followed aboard by numerous motorcycles, their riders and their passengers.

I found myself a seat in the passenger area and as I did so, the captain's voice crackled over the tannoy.

'Ladies and gentlemen, we are in for quite a rough passage today, and once we are underway I urge you all to remain seated. Thank you.'

Various passengers looked at each other wondering what to expect but the seasoned ferry-men and women looked unperturbed.

My seat had room for three people, and alongside it was a very tall, wide window which curved at its top and was moulded into the ceiling, with the bottom disappearing below my seat. There was the same three-seater opposite me with a small dining table in-between. I made myself comfortable and took a quick look at my fellow passengers, but my 'people-watching' was rudely interrupted.

A family of three large people appeared, mother and father and adult son, and they began in turn squeezing themselves into the seats opposite, issuing the odd grunt and wheeze as they did so. All of them were very well wrapped up in a variety of jumpers and cardigans and heavy coats and scarves and hats, even though it was quite warm.

I offered a cheery hello to my travel companions, but it was met with a stony silence and a funny look from 'Mother'. I looked out of the window and noticed that the clouds were very grey and heavy. A lady came over wearing a smart little uniform and a small hat and said there was a bar at the rear of the ferry if anyone fancied a bite to eat or a drink, but really we should stay in our seats. She had funny legs – sort of bandy – and when she walked away, she did so with a bandy gait.

The ferry got under way and we started to steam out of the harbour and into the Irish Sea, which was the colour of dark tea with white horses on top. I was quite amused and excited by the total contrast provided by this trip to service some school machines. Usually I had to sit in one of the vans in a traffic jam.

Ten or so minutes into the trip, I realised what the captain meant – the sea was extremely rough and the ferry was being thrown about like an overlooked coin in a washing machine. At various points when I looked out of the windows, we appeared to be underwater, and we were being badly buffeted as we climbed huge waves and then crashed down on the other side.

I began to experience a peculiar feeling in the pit of my stomach. Everyone remained in their seats, and more than a few were looking a tad pale, if not green – me included. The lady in the uniform appeared, walking down the aisle between the seats, and I could see her legs were like two springs absorbing all the shock and movement of the ferry. Her head, meanwhile, remained very still and she maintained a lovely smile as she walked from table to table asking if anyone needed a bag to be sick in. I declined her offer.

A spout of fervent chatter suddenly erupted amongst my three travel companions and then the mother struggled to her feet and, clinging to the seats and rails, made her way down the aisle.

Ten minutes later, Mother reappeared carrying a very large tray and bracing herself against seats and rails and people's heads and shoulders as she made her way back to her seat. She placed the tray on the table between us with, I noted, remarkably little spillage. The tray carried three huge hamburgers nestled inside three equally large bread buns and three large Coca Colas – with straws.

I began to feel hot and then cold and then nauseous and then hot and cold again. The son grabbed his burger and shoved it into his mouth and took a large bite. Mother and Father followed suit and soon the scene before me could only be described as one that resembled feeding time at the zoo.

All three of my companions chomped into their burgers and tomato ketchup and mayonnaise oozed between their fingers only for it to be licked clean in fear of losing the slightest morsel. Between their chomping, they would each take a long suck of their coca colas and the combination of hefty burger and bread and fizzy, sugary water soon had the effect of loud and unstifled belching.

I began to feel extremely unwell and slipped from my seat to find some air and some respite from the monkey cage. I staggered down the aisle and found a door, and pushing it open, was met by a cold blast of wind and water.

I stepped onto the deck outside and sheltered under a small overhang of some kind. All around, the sea was raging and boiling, and the ferry continued to be thrown around like a child's toy. However, the fresh sea air had an immediate effect on yours truly and I began to feel much better and quite exhilarated. I took several large breaths and normal service was resumed.

Casting my eye about me, I spotted a young woman sat on the soaking deck. She was wearing a black leather motorcycle suit from head to toe and a pair of short black boots with small silver-studded belts wrapped around them. She'd pulled up her knees to her chin and wrapped her arms around them. Her small face was very, very white, and her long blonde hair was blowing wildly in the gale. She was being soaked by the waves and the pouring rain, but I knew she felt absolutely awful with sea-sickness.

She caught my eye and I gave her a nod and pointed to the shelter where I was standing, but she shook her head gently as if to say to move would only make things worse.

A door by her side crashed open only inches from the girl as a burly young man appeared again wearing a black motorcycle suit and very heavy black boots. In one hand, he carried a pint of beer, and in the other another of the large hamburgers, and behind him was the bar containing several similarly dressed young men.

Spotting the young woman on the deck, he took a large bite of his burger and then swilled it down with an equally large gulp of his beer.

It appeared that they knew each other – maybe he was the boyfriend. He leaned down to the young woman and then shouted, 'What's wrong with you?' in a rather impatient and unpleasant manner. Flecks of burger and beer flew about her face as he spoke, and she turned away and drew in her legs and gripped them even tighter.

Getting no response from the girl, he stood back and spotted me, and I looked back at him with the best look of disapproval I could muster. He didn't appear to appreciate it and, clutching beer and burger, turned and went back through the doorway and into the bar, leaving the door to slam against the wall.

I stepped over and closed it and then went back to my place under the shelter. The girl was then violently sick across the small deck we shared, and when she'd finished I walked over and offered her my clean handkerchief, and she took it and attended to herself.

The sea began to ease and I spotted the Isle of Man before us and soon we were in calmer waters.

I drove off the ferry and headed for my hotel and the next day met the teacher and serviced her sewing machines.

The return sailing was uneventful and the sea was very calm and the ferry was almost empty. I managed to stay in my seat and even had a cup of tea. My mind drifted back to the young woman. I hoped she had phoned her mother and told her she was sorry and she had been right all along and she had told the boyfriend it

was all over.

In any event, I doubt if she, like me, will ever forget that trip.

HAMMERHEAD

I remember a day when my father was working in his workshop at home. It was a Sunday, one summer long ago, and it was warm in the workshop. I was about eight, and I stood quietly as I watched my father making a display cabinet for sewing machines for the shop. He was planing a length of timber – three by two – and at the end of each long stroke, the curled shavings fell onto the floor around our feet – and the wood smelled sweet.

Shafts of summer sun shining through the two small workshop windows lit up the tiny motes of wood dust as they danced in the air, rolling and rising and falling like small flies caught in the afternoon sunshine. The air hung heavy with the smells of the workshop and of fresh-cut timber and turpentine and paint. And in the far dark corners lay shovels and rakes.

He looked at me and gave me a wink, and I smiled back, proud that he was my daddy. He finished and stood, broad in the shoulder and deep in the chest, long in the leg and straight in the back.

My father had huge hands – hands made for work, plain and simple, honest and true. Each finger resembled a banana in size, and I noticed them most whenever he shook another man's hand. Their hands would disappear inside my father's mighty clasp and all you could see was their wrist poking out, like when the child shakes the hand of a man. And when they saw that, they knew.

He passed me the planer, which I took in my own two tiny hands, and asked for me to pass him his old hammer from his workbench. I was very happy to help my father and happy for him to ask for my help. It made me part of the show and part of the team, and I jumped to my task in double quick time.

Now he began to knock a line of nails into the timber. Each powerful stroke came down and he never missed a beat, and he never missed a nail, and each nail would sink deep – at the end of each blow. The bang of each blow made me feel dizzy, but I stood at my mark, watching each blow.

Then, as he raised the hammer, I saw a blur – something flying towards me. The head of the hammer had come loose from the shaft, and it was hurtling at speed towards my own small head.

A huge hand snapped out towards me like a striking cobra. My father had reached out and caught the hammer head mid-flight. He gave me a wink and he asked me to pass him another hammer, and we finished the job – together.

All is quiet in his workshop now – and the dust lies long settled.

Each tool in its place, and knowing its place – for their master is gone.

Printed in Great Britain
by Amazon